a gardening book: indoors and outdoors

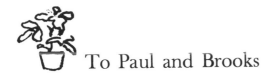 To Paul and Brooks

INTRODUCTION

This uncomplicated gardening book is filled with simple projects. In it, however, there are words used—and products called for—that may be unfamiliar to you. For example, let's say the directions call for *vermiculite.* The glossary in the back will tell what it means, and when you go to buy some, you will find that the florist or garden center person knows all about such things and will be quite impressed that you know about such things, too.

This book tells you also what kind of store sells which kinds of gardening things. Look in the section "Where To Buy Things."

The gardening projects in this book are most fun when done with somebody else. You will find that a cooperative grown-up is handy to have around when gardening in or out of doors. A grown-up is especially good at helping to dig, take cuttings, and lift things.

When you begin any of these projects, you might want to make a note of the date you planted the seeds or rooted the cuttings or whatever the first step is so that you will know when to start watching for something to happen.

Have fun, enjoy yourself, and may your garden flourish!

CONTENTS

Introduction   vii

Where To Buy Things   3

INDOORS   7

A Garden from Kitchen Scraps   9

Bean Sprouts, Alfalfa Sprouts, Chow Mein   19

A Windowsill Hodgepodge: Starting Plants from Seeds   26

Cuttings: Making New Plants from Old   33

Terrarium: An Indoor Woodland   41

An Avocado Tree   49

Cactus in a Colored Sand Painting   56

OUTDOORS   65

Salad Baskets   67

A Kitchen Garden   76

An Herb Garden   90

Glossary   99

a gardening book: indoors and outdoors

WHERE TO BUY THINGS

PEBBLES AND SAND

Coarse Sand
Garden centers, some dime stores, and some hardware stores

Colored Fine Sand
Dime stores and pet shops that sell aquarium equipment, some florists and garden centers

Pebbly Sand
Dime stores and pet shops that sell aquarium equipment, some florists and garden centers

Pebbles and Marble Chips
Garden centers, some dime stores, and some hardware stores

PLANTS

VEGETABLE

Green Peppers
Tomatoes
Garden centers, greenhouses, some hardware stores, and some dime stores

FLOWERS

Marigolds
Garden centers, greenhouses, some hardware stores, and some dime stores

HERBS

Basil
Chives
Garden centers, greenhouses, some hardware stores. Chive plants

Thyme
Parsley

are sometimes sold in grocery
stores

CACTUS

Garden centers, greenhouses,
florists, dime stores

TERRARIUM

Ferns
Mosses
Ivy
and other tiny plants

Florists, garden centers, greenhouses, and some dime stores

SEEDS

FLOWER AND VEGETABLE

Beet
Bush Bean
Carrot
Loose-leaf Lettuce

Nasturtium
Radish
Sweet Corn
Zucchini

Garden centers, hardware stores,
dime stores, some grocery stores

SEEDS FOR SPROUTS

Alfalfa

Health food and natural food
stores

Mung Bean

Natural food stores, Chinese and
Japanese markets

SOIL: POTTING AND PLANTER

All-Purpose Potting Soil
Cactus Soil
Planter Soil
Terrarium Soil

Garden centers, some hardware
stores, and some dime stores

TOOLS

Hand Cultivator (claw)
Hoe
Hose
Rake
Spade
Spray Nozzle (for hose)

Garden centers, hardware stores,
lawn and garden equipment centers

Rotary Tiller

Rental service stores, some lawn
and garden equipment centers

MISCELLANY

Charcoal

Dime stores, pet shops

Cheese Cloth

Hardware stores, dime stores

Chow Mein Noodles

Grocery stores

Fertilizer (water soluble)

Hardware stores, dime stores,
garden centers, and some florists

Fungicide

Garden centers, hardware stores

Garden Markers

Garden centers, hardware stores

Gloves (work and rubber)

Dime stores, hardware stores, some
garden centers and grocery stores

Insecticides	Garden centers, hardware stores, some dime stores
Manure	Garden centers, some hardware stores
Peat Moss	Garden centers, some hardware stores, dime stores, and florists
Perlite	Garden centers, some hardware stores, dime stores, and florists
Plastic Bags (trash and sandwich)	Grocery stores, hardware stores
Rooting Agent	Garden centers, some hardware stores, and some dime stores
Sphagnum Moss	Garden centers, some hardware stores, dime stores, and florists
Stakes (wooden and bamboo)	Garden centers, hardware stores, some dime stores
Sprayers (atomizers, bulb, misters)	Garden centers, dime stores, hardware stores
Styrofoam Cups	Dime stores, grocery stores
Vermiculite	Garden centers, some hardware stores, some dime stores, and florists

INDOORS

A GARDEN
FROM KITCHEN SCRAPS

A CARROT TOP DISH-GARDEN

This may be a beet top or a turnip top or an all-three-together garden. It is just about the quickest, the easiest, and the least expensive garden in the world, and what is even better than that—it's pretty.

THINGS YOU WILL NEED

1. A bright spot not in the direct sun

2. Carrots (or beets, or turnips, or all three)

3. Pebbles, gravel, or sand

4. A shallow dish or bowl (cereal-bowl size or larger)

5. A sharp knife and one helpful grown-up to use it

6. Old newspapers

7. Water

MAKING THE GARDEN

1. Spread out some old newspapers where you plan to make your dish-garden and gather together all the things you will need.

2. Put a layer of pebbles (or sand or gravel) in the bottom of a shallow dish.

3. If the carrots (or beets or turnips) have stems and leaves, cut them off and throw them away. Next, cut about 1 inch off the top of each of the vegetables you are going to use.

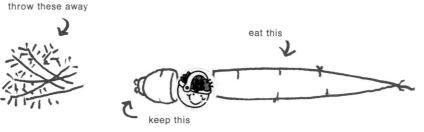

throw these away

eat this

keep this

4. Put the tops in the dish on top of the pebbles.

5. Pour water into the dish so it covers the pebbles. About ¼ inch of the vegetable tops also should be covered by water.

6. Put the dish in a bright spot, but not in the direct sun.

7. Add a little water to the dish each day to replace any that has evaporated.

In a week or two fresh new leaves will sprout from the vegetable tops. Soon after that the carrot leaves will start to resemble feathery ferns. Beet and turnip tops will sprout broad leaves. They don't look like ferns but are nice in their own special way.

A SWEET POTATO VINE

An old sweet potato in your mother's vegetable bin can become an important member of your household.

This is a plant that grows and grows and grows. If you tack up strings for it, it will grow around a window or all around a room or all around just about anywhere it can get some light. It's a very cheerful plant to have around.

THINGS YOU WILL NEED

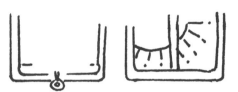

1. A well-shaded place away from direct sunlight and, later, a place with bright sunlight

2. An old (yet unspoiled) sweet potato with little buds on it

3. 4 toothpicks

4. A one-quart jar

5. Little pieces of charcoal (the kind used in aquariums)

6. Water

STARTING THE SWEET POTATO

1. Fill the quart jar, not quite to the top, with water. Add a few small pieces of charcoal to the water to keep it sweet.

2. Poke 4 toothpicks partway into the sweet potato, in a line around the middle.

3. Put the sweet potato in the jar, resting the toothpicks on the rim. The end with the most buds is usually the top of a sweet potato; the part with a small, flat scar, where the sweet potato was cut from its stem, is the bottom. The bottom part should be under water.

4. Put the sweet potato, jar and all, in a well-shaded area until roots grow from the bottom and vines begin to sprout from the top. This growth will start in anywhere from a few days to a few weeks.

5. Add a little lukewarm water to the jar every 2 or 3 days.

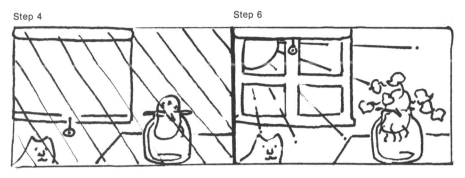

6. When vines and roots begin to appear, move the sweet
   potato to a bright, sunny spot.

If you like, you can replant your sweet potato in a pot a
month or two after the vines first sprout. If you do, the vine
will grow more vigorously.

How to Pot Your Sweet Potato Vine

**THINGS YOU WILL NEED
(to plant the potato)**

1. A sweet potato vine

2. A sunny place

3. A deep, roomy flowerpot (its height
   should be twice the length of the
   fleshy part of the potato. If your
   potato is 5 inches long, the pot
   should be at least 10 inches tall)

4. A saucer or dish to go under the pot

5. Potting soil (the store-bought kind is good for growing sweet potatoes)

6. Pebbles or gravel

7. Water-soluble fertilizer

8. Old newspapers

POTTING THE SWEET POTATO VINE

1. Spread out the newspapers where you plan to do the planting.

2. Sprinkle a layer of pebbles or gravel on the bottom of the flowerpot for good drainage.

3. Fill the flowerpot within an inch or so of the top with potting soil.

4. Scoop a hole in the soil deep enough to hold the length of the sweet potato. Put the potato in the hole and press the soil firmly around it.

5. Water the plant thoroughly until the water runs from the drainage hole in the bottom of the pot.

6. Put the plant in a sunny place.

TENDING THE SWEET POTATO VINE

1. Water it once or twice a week. The soil should be kept moist.

2. Fertilize it every month or two, using a water-soluble fertilizer. Follow the instructions on the fertilizer package.

Put the plant on a high shelf or hang it from a plant holder and see how long it takes for the vines to reach the floor; or tack up strings for the vines to climb on; or wrap the vines around and around the pot; or snip off the ends of the vines to keep them a length that pleases you. There are endless possibilities.

BEAN SPROUTS,
ALFALFA SPROUTS, CHOW MEIN

Homegrown sprouts are crisp and crunchy—better than the ones that come in cans. They will grow in your kitchen in less than a week, and you will have homegrown vegetables all year round.

Bean Sprouts

THINGS YOU WILL NEED

1. A warm, dark place (a kitchen cabinet is perfect)

2. 3 tablespoons of mung beans (these will grow into a cup or more of sprouts)

3. A piece of cheesecloth at least 6 inches square

4. 1 rubber band

5. 1 quart jar (an old mayonnaise or jelly jar is fine)

6. 1 medium-to-fine sieve

7. 1 bowl (a cereal bowl is fine)

HOW TO SPROUT THEM

1. Measure out 3 tablespoons of mung beans into a bowl.

2. Pick out all the broken and shriveled beans and throw them away.

3. Put those that are left in a sieve and wash them well under running water.

4. Now place the beans in the bowl, cover them with water, and let them soak overnight.

5. The next day, drain the beans, using the sieve, and then give them a good rinsing.

6. Put the beans in the jar. Cover the top with a double layer of cheesecloth. Slip the rubber band over the cheesecloth to hold it firmly in place.

7. Hold the jar on its side and shake it gently, so the beans will spread out into a single layer.

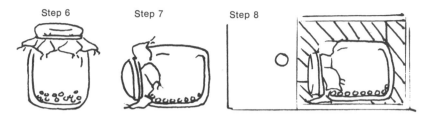

Step 6   Step 7   Step 8

8. Keeping the jar on its side, put it in a warm, dark place.

9. Rinse the beans 3 times a day, every day, and drain them well each time so they won't get moldy. To do this, put the top of the jar under a water tap, fill it with cool water, give it a couple of swirls, then drain the water out through the cheesecloth. After draining, hold the jar on its side and give it a few shakes to separate the beans so they won't grow together in a tight tangle. Then put the jar back in its dark place, lying on its side.

10. The bean sprouts will be ready when they have reached the length of 1½–2½ inches. This usually takes three to five days. When they are ready, put them in a sieve,

Step 9

rinse them under a tap, remove the loosened little green skins, and drain them well. At this point the sprouts are ready to eat. You will now have more than a cup of these delicious things.

The sooner you eat the sprouts the better, but they will keep in the refrigerator for a few days if you put them in a plastic bag or covered dish.

Alfalfa Sprouts

Alfalfa seeds sprout the same way as beans do, but you will need only one tablespoon of alfalfa seeds and a pint, rather than a quart, jar to sprout them in. Keep the jar in a warm, dark place and rinse the same way as you do the bean sprouts. These sprouts will be ready to eat in about three or four days when they are 1-inch long. At this point put them in a sieve, rinse them under a tap, and rinse away the loosened seed coatings. Drain the sprouts well. They are now ready to eat.

If you would like these sprouts to turn green, place the jar in a sunny window when the first leaves pop out of the seeds, and continue to rinse three times a day.

GOOD WAYS TO EAT BEAN AND ALFALFA SPROUTS

Bean sprouts are fat and crunchy and, when raw, taste a little like green beans. Alfalfa sprouts are light and feathery and taste a bit like peas. Both are good to munch on just as they are for a snack. You can toss them in a mixed salad, or tuck them in a sandwich, or sprinkle them on soup, or cook them in a delicious dish, like chow mein.

Crispy Chicken Chow Mein

THINGS YOU WILL NEED

1 grown-up to help you cook
     and

Ingredients

2 tablespoons vegetable oil
3 medium onions, chopped
1 cup sliced mushrooms
3 cups chopped celery
2 cups of chicken broth
2 tablespoons soy sauce
2 teaspoons arrowroot, mixed in ¼ cup
     of water until smooth
2 cups of cooked chicken, cut in thin
     strips
1 cup of bean sprouts (sprouted from 3
     tablespoons of mung beans)

1 or 2 cans of chow mein noodles or
  cooked rice
Alfalfa sprouts (a sprinkling of these on
  top of the chow mein is an *optional*
  final touch)

HOW TO COOK

1. Heat the oil in a skillet and gently fry the onions until they are transparent. Add the celery and mushrooms, and cook for two minutes.

2. Stir in the soy sauce and chicken broth. Bring to a boil.

3. Lower the heat, and briskly stir in the arrowroot and water mixture.

4. Add the chicken and bean sprouts, and cook until they are heated through and the sauce has thickened slightly.

5. Serve over warm chow mein noodles or hot rice.

6. If you would like to make this dish even prettier, sprinkle some alfalfa sprouts on top of it just before serving.

A WINDOWSILL HODGEPODGE
Starting Plants from Seeds

Here's a good thing to do. Plant some nasturtium, corn, and bean seeds, water them, put them in a sunny window, and they will turn into a hodgepodge windowsill garden.

When they are grown, here's what they'll do for you. The nasturtiums will bloom with orange and yellow flowers most of the year. The bean plants will produce some flowers and a green bean or two. The corn will grow green and hand- some. (It won't grow any ears indoors, but probably it would like to.)

THINGS YOU WILL NEED

1. A windowsill or a similar sunny area

2. 6 styrofoam drinking cups

3. Clean pebbles

4. Seeds: 1 packet each of nasturtium, bush bean, and sweet corn

5. Enough shallow dishes or foil frozen food trays to hold the styrofoam cups

6. Water and a watering can

7. Water-soluble fertilizer

8. Old newspapers

9. A pencil or a large nail

10. 1 package of store-bought potting soil or *homemade potting mixture,* which consists of:

   4 cups of vermiculite or perlite
   2 cups of sand
   (Use a large bowl or a bucket to mix them in.)

Some people like homemade potting soil better than the store-bought kind for a couple of reasons. One, because it drains so well that it makes overwatering and drowning a plant almost impossible. The other is that plants grown in it are much less likely to be damaged by fungus.

Store-bought potting soil is handy, however, because it comes ready to use and plants growing in it do not need fertilizing as often as those growing in the homemade kind.

GETTING READY

1. Gather together all the things you will need. (You won't need the fertilizer until the seeds are well sprouted, in 10 days to 3 weeks.)

2. Spread out the newspapers and, if you are making home-made potting soil, make it now. Mix the ingredients together with a little water in a large bowl or bucket. Use just enough water to moisten the soil lightly.

3. Poke 3 or 4 small drainage holes in the bottom of each styrofoam cup. A pencil or large nail is good for doing this.

4. Sprinkle an inch or two of pebbles on the bottom of each cup.

5. Fill the cups, not quite to the top, with potting soil. Lightly press down the soil to make it level.

poking seeds into soil

PLANTING

Step 3

1. Use two cups for each kind of seed.

2. To plant the nasturtiums, use your finger to poke 4 to 6 seeds a half-inch deep into the soil of each cup.

3. To plant the beans, poke 2 or 3 seeds about one inch deep into the soil of each cup. Do the same with the corn.

4. Press the soil down firmly, filling in the holes where the seeds are planted.

5. Water the seeds gently by slowly pouring water around the inside rim of each cup. This way of watering keeps the seeds from becoming buried too deeply. Keep pouring until the water streams from the drainage holes in the bottoms of the cups.

6. Put the cups in the shallow dish or aluminum food trays and place in a windowsill or any other place that gets lots of sun.

7. Water thoroughly every day.

Step 1

TENDING THE PLANTS

1. In 10 days to 3 weeks little green seedlings will start to show above the soil. If you have used homemade potting soil, start using fertilizer one month after the seedlings first appear, not before. Fertilizing too early can kill a plant.

   If you have used store-bought potting soil, wait 6 to 8 weeks after the seedlings have first appeared before using fertilizer.

   In preparing the fertilizer follow the instructions on the fertilizer package.

2. From this point on, fertilize plants growing in home-made potting soil once a week. Plants growing in store-bought soil should be fertilized only once a month.

3. From the time seedlings appear, water every 3 days or when the plants begin to look a little bit droopy. Do not water them more frequently than this. More plants are killed by too much water than by not getting enough.

4. Remember, plants are like people and don't like being too close to radiators or sitting in draughty places, and they, too, enjoy being loved and admired.

5. The bean plants will be the first to come into bloom, about one month after planting, and little beans will soon follow. Pinch off withered blossoms and shriveled beans.

    The corn will grow green and a foot or so tall. It does not flower. The nasturtiums will, at first, grow more and more leaves and after a few months will start producing flowers. Pinch off the blossoms when they wither.

6. The nasturtiums can be moved to larger pots when they look too big for the ones in which they were started. Beans and corn do not transplant well, so if you wish to have them growing all year round, plant new cups of seeds every two months or so.

CUTTINGS
Making New Plants from Old

Start new plants from your own old favorites or from a friend's pretty plant. Cuttings can be snipped from a flourishing mature plant without harming it. You can grow new plants from these cuttings. It is a wonderful way to enlarge your indoor garden.

THINGS YOU WILL NEED

1. A sunny window

2. 1 or more mature plants (such as begonias, geraniums, coleus, ivy, or carnations)

3. 8 clear plastic sandwich bags

4. 8 rubber bands

5. 8 styrofoam cups

6. 1 pencil or large nail

7. Enough shallow dishes or frozen food trays to hold the styrofoam cups

8. 1 refillable sprayer (Windex bottle, or bulb sprayer, atomizer, etc.)

9. 4 cups peat moss

10. 4 cups sand

11. Rooting agent
    (to help roots to grow)

12. 1 large bowl or bucket

13. Lots of old newspapers

14. Water

15. 1 very sharp knife or razor blade
    plus an adult to use it

16. Water-soluble fertilizer

GETTING READY

1. Spread out newspapers where you plan to work.

2. Have all the things you need at hand.

3. With the pencil or nail poke 4 drainage holes in the
   bottom of each cup.

4. Measure 4 cups of sand and 4 cups of peat moss into
   the large bowl or bucket. Mix well. Use a styrofoam cup

to measure and your hands to mix. Gradually add water until the mixture is completely damp.

5. Fill the cups to the rim with the sand and peat moss mixture. Don't pack it down. Put the cups in the dishes or trays quickly—they leak!

6. Now you will need an adult with a sure hand and a sharp knife or razor blade. Ask her or him to take 8 cuttings from the mature plant or plants you have chosen.

TAKING CUTTINGS

1. With the knife or razor blade, cut 3 or more inches off the top of a plant stem just below a leaf joint.

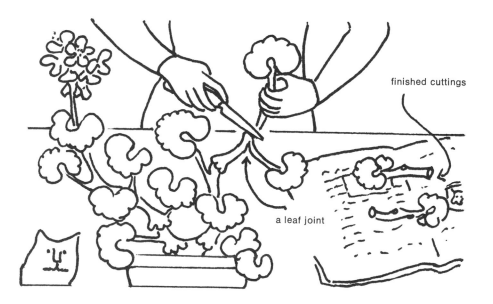

finished cuttings

a leaf joint

2. Remove the lower leaves from the cutting, leaving only 2 or 3 small leaves at the top.

3. Spread out the cuttings on a clean newspaper. (Cuttings can be kept a day or two in the refrigerator if wrapped well in plastic wrap. This is handy to know if you wish to take cuttings from a friend's plant or a garden plant. Just before planting, cut a thin slice from the bottom of each cutting.)

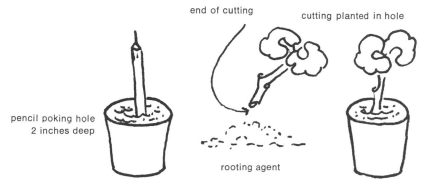

pencil poking hole 2 inches deep

end of cutting

cutting planted in hole

rooting agent

PLANTING THE CUTTINGS

1. At the center of each cup, poke a hole 2 inches deep in the sand and peat moss mixture. Use the unsharpened end of a pencil to do this.

2. Dip the end of the cutting in the rooting agent and then plant it in one of the holes you have made in the sand and peat moss mixture. Secure the cutting by gently pressing down the mixture surrounding it. Plant each cutting this way—1 to a cup—until all are planted.

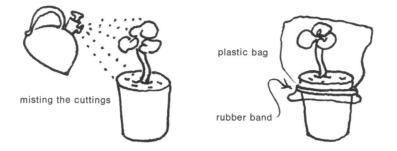

misting the cuttings

plastic bag

rubber band

3. Water each cutting slowly and gently until water drips from the drainage holes in the bottom of the cup.

4. Using the sprayer, mist the cuttings with water. Spray just enough to give the effect of morning dew.

5. Carefully slip a plastic sandwich bag over the top of each of the planted cups. Now, secure each plastic bag with a rubber band. Each cutting is now in its own private greenhouse!

6. Place the planted cuttings in the shallow dishes or trays and put them in a sunny window, or if the weather is hot or summery, 2 or 3 feet back from a window. Leave them there 3 weeks. During these 3 weeks there is no need to water or tend the cuttings.

7. Three weeks after planting, remove the plastic bags from the cups, and test the cuttings by tugging them very, very gently. If they resist, that means they have taken root and that the plastic bags should remain off. The cuttings will look a little sad and droopy at this

tugging very gently

point, so water them well, mist them 2 or 3 times during their first day without bags, and pinch off any of the leaves that have turned yellow. If, however, the cuttings come loose when you test them, pat the soil back down around them, water them well, mist them, and slip the bags back over them. Secure the bags with rubber bands, and put the cuttings back in the window. Test them again 1 week later. Some plants take a little longer to root than others.

TENDING THE NEW PLANTS

1. Once the cuttings have rooted, they are no longer cuttings, but new plants.

2. Three days after you have removed the plastic bags, water the plants with a water-soluble fertilizer, following the directions on the package.

3. Fertilize the plants once a month.

4. Keep the plants in a sunny place.

5. Water the plants when the soil feels dry. You might try talking to them!

TERRARIUM
An Indoor Woodland

Imagine a mysterious miniature woodland world where winding paths seem to disappear and tiny plants look like towering trees. You can make one for yourself. Here's how.

THINGS YOU WILL NEED

1. A glass or plastic container with a wide mouth (a candy jar, pickle or peanut butter jar, a brandy snifter, a fishbowl, an aquarium, or perhaps a container designed to be a terrarium)

2. A glass lid or piece of glass, plastic, or plastic kitchen wrap (someone at a hardware store or a glazier can cut a piece of glass or plastic to fit your container).

3. A package of terrarium soil or homemade terrarium soil, which consists of:

   1 part potting soil
   1 part coarse sand
   1 part shredded peat moss
   (Use a large bowl or bucket to mix them in)

4. Several tiny plants. You can buy mosses, ferns, tiny evergreen or

palm trees, ivy, baby's tears ,etc.; or you can gather small plants from your backyard or a nearby field. If you gather plants, you will need a trowel or a large metal spoon for digging, some paper cups or plastic sandwich bags to put the plants in, and a carton for carrying the plants home.

Dig up a large ball of soil with each plant to protect the roots. Put each plant in a separate paper cup or plastic bag to protect the roots further and to keep them from drying out. Carry the plants home in a carton. When at home, sprinkle them well with water. This is especially important if you are not planning to plant your terrarium right away.

Don't mix the wild and store-bought plants together. The hardy wild plants may carry a fungus or insect that could harm more delicate store-bought plants.

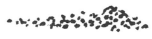

5. Charcoal (the kind used in aquariums)

6. Pebbles, marble chips, or coarse sand

7. Shredded peat moss or sphagnum moss

8. Small interesting things (stones, shells, bits of wood, or perhaps a ceramic frog or snail)

9. Pebbly sand (the kind used in aquariums—smaller and prettier than the regular pebbles)

10. A watercolor paintbrush

11. A long-handled spoon (an ice-tea spoon will do)

12. A spray mister or bulb sprayer

13. Old newspapers

GETTING READY

1. Gather together all the things you will need and spread out the newspapers where you plan to work.

2. Wash the container in warm soapy water. Rinse it and dry it well.

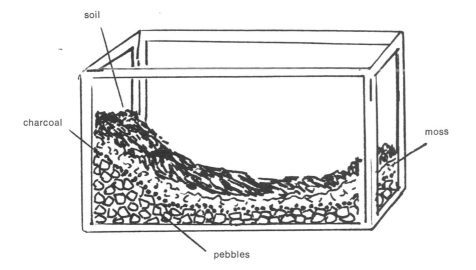

soil

charcoal

moss

pebbles

3. Cover the bottom of the container with pebbles, marble chips, or coarse sand. About an inch or two should be enough for good drainage. For a more interesting landscape, make a little hill or two with the pebbles, chips, or coarse sand.

4. Scatter a thin layer of charcoal, about ¼- to ½-inch thick, over the sand, chips, or pebbles to keep the terrarium fresh and sweet. The charcoal absorbs the fumes and odors caused by the natural decay that takes place in warm, moist places.

5. Now, add a layer of moistened sphagnum moss or shredded peat moss. One-half to 1 inch should do.

6. Cover the moss with 2 or 3 inches of soil.

PLANTING THE TERRARIUM

1. Now is a good time to decide which of the little plants you have gathered together will look best in your terrarium. Choose at least one of the taller ones and let that be a tree. Use a little moss for the forest floor and perhaps a miniature fern to serve as underbrush.

2. If you are using potted plants, take them out of their pots. Dig little holes in the terrarium soil with the long-handled spoon. The holes should be just deep enough to hold the plants' roots. Put a plant in each hole and press the soil firmly around them, using a finger or the back of the spoon. If the plants look as though they need more soil to hold them upright, spoon more around them, then press it down. Mosses don't need holes—simply press them into the soil.

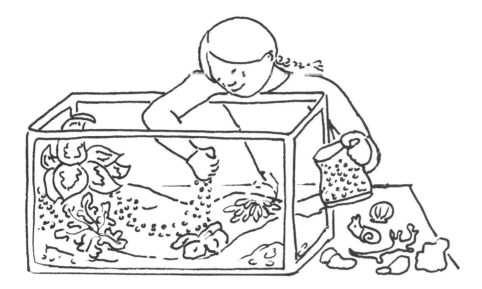

FINISHING TOUCHES

1. Carefully sprinkle a winding path of the pebbly sand and add whatever interesting small things you have chosen— some stones, a shell, a ceramic frog—whatever suits your fancy.

2. When everything is in place, brush away any soil that may have collected on the glass of the terrarium. A watercolor paintbrush is good for doing this.

3. Water the plants well, using a spray mister or a bulb sprinkler. Stop spraying when the water begins to seep down into the layer of coarse sand or pebbles at the bottom.

4. When all the water has evaporated off the inside walls of the terrarium, cover it with its own glass lid, plastic wrap, or a piece of glass or clear plastic.

5. Keep the terrarium out of the direct sunlight. It can even be in a shady place.

TENDING THE TERRARIUM

If the terrarium becomes foggy, open the lid partway or take it off completely. In hot, humid weather you will probably need to keep the terrarium uncovered or just partway covered most of the time.

Water your terrarium once a month, at the most, using a spray mister or bulb sprinkler. If the terrarium is cloudy or wet in the mornings, it does not need to be watered. Some terrariums have thrived for years without being watered at all.

Take out any leaves or plants that may die. You can replace these if you like or leave the space for the new growth of the remaining plants.

Wipe the terrarium, inside and out, from time to time to keep it sparkling clean.

AN AVOCADO TREE

Eat a couple of avocados (nice ripe ones). Save the pits, sprout them, plant them, grow them into trees, and your house will begin to look like the jungly tropics.

THINGS YOU WILL NEED

1. 1 or 2 avocado pits—some refuse to sprout, so it's best to start with two.

2. A warm, dark place away from drafts (a kitchen cabinet, perhaps)

3. Wooden toothpicks (the strong, rounded kind)

4. A glass at least 5 inches tall

ROOTING AND SPROUTING THE PIT

1. Rinse the pit in lukewarm water. While rinsing it, peel off any loose pieces of the skin that covers the pit. Dry the pit carefully with a paper towel and rub off any remaining loose skin.

2. Push 3 or 4 toothpicks into the pit, in a line around its middle. Avocado pits are quite hard, so somebody with a strong hand is needed to do this.

Steps 1 and 2

3. Fill the glass with lukewarm water and put the pit in it, resting the toothpicks on the rim. The water should cover the bottom of the pit by at least a half-inch. (The bottom is the fat, dimpled end.)

4. Now put the pit, glass and all, in a dark, warm place.

5. Check the water level of the glass every few days. The bottom half-inch of the pit should always be in water. Add lukewarm water to the glass as needed.

6. Signs of growth will appear any time from a few days to a month. First a root will show itself, and the pit will split. Later—there's no telling when—a green shoot will poke

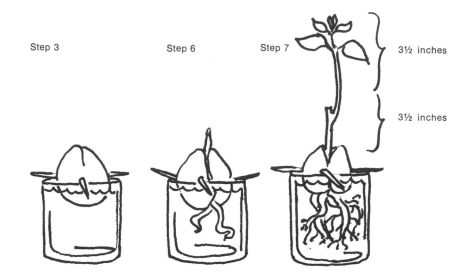

Step 3   Step 6   Step 7   3½ inches

3½ inches

out at the top. Soon after that little leaves will appear. Continue to keep the sprouting pit in a warm, dark place until it is ready to pot.

7. Let the shoot grow until it is 7 inches high, then cut off the top 3½ inches. Use sharp scissors to do this. Cutting the stem in half like this makes some people feel very nervous. But if the stem is not cut, the shoot will grow into a scrawny stick with only a few sad leaves.

The pit will be ready to plant in a pot when new growth appears on the cut stem and the roots have thickened a little and grown almost long enough to touch the bottom of the glass.

Some avocado pits won't sprout no matter how tenderly you care for them. So if yours hasn't shown signs of life within

Step 7

a month or two, or if the water becomes cloudy and has a nasty smell, toss it out. Then eat another avocado and start again.

**THINGS YOU WILL NEED
(to plant the pit)**

1. A large flowerpot (one with a top diameter of 10½ inches would be good)

2. Pebbles or gravel

3. a 10-pound bag of potting soil

4. 6 cups of vermiculite

An Avocado Tree   53

5. A bucket or large mixing bowl

6. A bamboo or wooden stick about 3 feet tall

7. A dish to put under the pot

8. Old newspapers

PLANTING

1. Gather together all the things you need and spread out lots of old newspapers to work on.

2. Mix the potting soil and vermiculite together in the bucket or large bowl.

3. Put a layer or two of pebbles or gravel in the bottom of the pot. Now, fill the pot almost to the top with the potting soil and vermiculite mix.

4. In the middle of the pot, scoop a hole in the soil deep enough to hold the roots of the pit. Pull the toothpicks out of the pit. If some are stubborn, just snap them off. Plant the pit in the hole, leaving the top half of the pit uncovered. Press the soil down very gently. Then push the bamboo or wooden stick through the soil until it reaches the bottom of the pot. The stick should be about 2 inches away from the pit.

5. Water the avocado thoroughly, using lukewarm water. Pour the water very slowly and carefully. Keep pouring until the water runs from the drainage hole in the bottom of the pot.

6. Now, place the potted avocado on a dish in a sunny spot.

TENDING THE AVOCADO TREE

1. Water the tree daily, always using lukewarm water. Avocado trees thrive in moist soil, so overwatering is not a worry.

2. A week or two after potting, fertilize the plant with a water-soluble fertilizer, following the instructions on the fertilizer package. After that, fertilize it once a month.

3. To keep the tree from getting scrawny, pinch off any new top growth. Start doing this after the tree is 2 or 3 feet tall.

   When the tree reaches the height of 5 to 7 feet, repot it in a larger pot. Avocado trees can grow ceiling-high; cutting off the top growth will keep your tree from outgrowing your house.

   Avocado trees won't bear fruit indoors, but they are so beautiful, no one really minds.

CACTUS IN A COLORED SAND PAINTING

(Inspired by the Navajo Indians)

Sand paintings in glass jars are very easy to make but look as though they are very, very difficult. People who don't know the secret of making them marvel at them. And when they see a cactus growing out of the top of a sand painting, they marvel all the more!

THINGS YOU WILL NEED

1. A bright place, not in the direct sun

2. A small cactus

3. A tall glass container (choose one about twice as tall as the pot the cactus came in. You can use a tall water tumbler, a brandy snifter, a glass food storage jar, a large peanut butter jar, a small fishbowl, etc.)

4. 3 or more bags of colored fine sand (the kind sold to put in goldfish bowls or terrariums)

5. Some small pretty pebbles

6. A small package of store-bought cactus soil or homemade cactus soil which consists of:

Cactus in a Colored Sand Painting   57

1 part potting soil
1 part perlite or coarse sand
1 part shredded peat moss
(use a bowl to mix them in)

7. A pencil or a small paintbrush

8. Heavy work gloves or rubber gloves

9. Old newspapers

10. Water

GETTING READY

1. Gather together all the things you will need and spread out the newspapers in the area where you are going to sand-paint and plant.

2. If the container you are planning to use is not already sparkly clean, wash it in warm soapy water, rinse it, and dry it well.

MAKING A SAND PAINTING IN A GLASS CONTAINER

1. Snip off one corner of each little bag of colored sand that you plan to use.

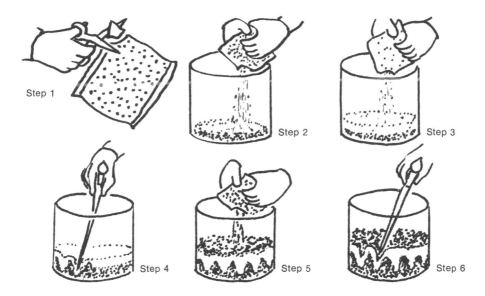

Step 1

Step 2

Step 3

Step 4

Step 5

Step 6

2. Choose the color you want to have at the bottom of your sand painting. Then, pour some of that sand into the bottom of the jar, making a layer about an inch deep.

3. Gently pour a layer of the next color over it.

4. Now start to make a design by pushing down the sand with the pointed end of a pencil or the handle end of a small paintbrush.

5. Next pour in a different color of sand and, using the pencil or brush handle, continue making the design. Stop the sand painting when your container is half-full in order to leave room for the cactus.

6. You might like to make a landscape sand painting. Here are some ideas for one.

Pour in a layer of green sand for grass, top it with a layer of blue to make a river, add more green for more grass. Then, make some hills in purple or natural-colored sand by pouring the sand quite thickly in some places and quite thinly in others. Now, pour in more blue until the hilltops are covered. This is the beginning of the sky. You can make a cloud or two by spooning a little natural or white sand up against the glass. Again add blue, but do this very carefully so you do not disturb the clouds. If you would like to have a bird flying in the sky, spoon about one-quarter of a teaspoon of dark sand next to the glass. Then with a sharp pencil, push it down in the middle, just a little bit. Now very carefully add more blue sand to complete the sky.

PLANTING THE CACTUS

1. If you are not using packaged cactus soil, mix up a little of the homemade kind in a bowl.

2. Spoon an inch or two of cactus soil into the glass container right on top of your sand painting.

3. Put on some rubber gloves or heavy work gloves to protect your hands from cactus pricklers. Take the cactus out of the pot it has been growing in. To do this, gently hold the cactus in the palm of one gloved hand. Take the pot firmly with the other hand and turn the pot and cactus upside down. Lift the pot off the cactus. If the pot does not come away easily, rap the rim of the pot against the edge of a table, still holding the cactus

upside down. Rap it a couple of times and then lift the pot off the cactus.

4. Now put the cactus into the container. Cover the roots with cactus soil. Press down the soil gently but firmly around the cactus. You can take off those gloves now.

5. Scatter a few pretty pebbles around the cactus and move the container to a bright place out of the direct rays of the sun.

TENDING THE CACTUS

These prickly little plants need very little care—they don't like being fussed over.

WATERING

Between November and February, your cactus needs a good watering only every three or four weeks at the most. Cacti are in a semidormant (sleeping) state during these winter months and need just enough water to keep from shriveling up.

The rest of the year, water them about every two weeks. The soil should be quite dry before you water. If the soil seems moist, wait a few days until it dries out and then water.

Water the cactus only on bright, sunny days. If cacti are watered during muggy, damp weather, their roots are likely to rot.

FERTILIZING

Fertilize your cactus once a year in the springtime. Use a water-soluble fertilizer, following the directions on the package.

Keep your cactus-in-a-sand-painting somewhere where everybody can see it and marvel at it.

OUTDOORS

SALAD BASKETS

Grow lettuce, radishes, tomatoes, and green peppers in half-bushel baskets. Put them on your doorstep, terrace, balcony—anywhere they will get some sun.

THINGS YOU WILL NEED

1. A sunny or partially shaded spot such as a terrace, doorstep, or balcony

2. Old newspapers

3. 4 half-bushel baskets

4. 4 plastic trash can bags (kitchen size 24″ x 20″ x 20″)

5. A pencil or big nail

6. Pebbles

7. A bag of planter soil (2 bushels or 4 cubic feet)

8. 1 packet loose-leaf lettuce seeds

9. 1 packet radish seeds

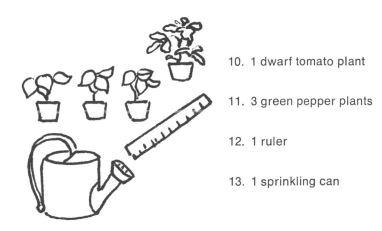

10. 1 dwarf tomato plant

11. 3 green pepper plants

12. 1 ruler

13. 1 sprinkling can

GETTING READY TO PLANT

1. Gather together all the things you will need.

2. Using a pencil or a big nail, poke 8 drainage holes in the bottom of each of the plastic bags.

3. Line the baskets with the plastic bags.

4. Put down a couple of layers of pebbles in the bottom of each plastic bag for good drainage.

5. Fill the bags within 2 inches of the top with planter soil.

trash bag lining basket

bird's-eye view of
freshly planted baskets

Planting

THE RADISH BASKET

Use a stick or your finger to make straight furrows ½ inch
deep (see seed packet for distance between rows). Plant
the radish seeds 1 inch apart in the furrows. Cover the
seeds with soil and press down firmly. Water well (until the
water seeps from the bottom of the basket). Use a
sprinkling can and water very slowly to prevent the seeds
from being too deeply buried to grow.

THE LETTUCE BASKET

For the lettuce make furrows ¼ inch deep (see seed packet for distance between rows). Scatter the seeds lightly in each furrow. Cover the seeds with soil and press down firmly. Water them the same way as the radishes. Lettuce grows nicely in partial shade.

THE DWARF TOMATO PLANT

Right in the middle of the basket scoop a hole deep enough to hold the full length of the roots of the plant, no deeper. Put the plant in the hole and press the soil firmly around it. Sprinkle well until the water seeps from the bottom of the basket. Tomatoes need lots of sun.

THE THREE GREEN PEPPER PLANTS

Scoop out three holes in the soil an equal distance from each other and a few inches in from the basket rim. Plant and water the green peppers the same way as the tomato plant. Peppers, too, need full sun.

bird's-eye view
of holes to plant
green peppers in

Tending the Salad Baskets

WATERING

Give the baskets a good watering when the top ⅛ inch of the soil is dry. If the weather is hot and dry, water the vegetables 3 times a week.

FERTILIZING

Fertilize the plants every 3 weeks. Follow the directions on the fertilizer package.

THINNING

Thin the radish seedlings so they are 1 inch apart. The lettuce plants should be 4 to 6 inches apart. Thin the lettuce when the leaves are still small, but large enough to eat. They will make a delicious salad.

WEEDS AND PESTS

Weed the baskets often. Weeds harbor bugs and use up the nutrients the vegetables need. If insects or fungus attack the plants, use a pesticide or fungicide made especially for vegetable gardens—others may be poisonous.

THE HARVEST

The radishes and lettuce should be ready to eat about 1 month after planting. Pick lettuce leaves as you need them. The tomatoes and peppers will be ready in 2 months or more.

A GARDEN-PLANNING CHART

PLANTS

(showing the distance needed
between plants and between rows)

Tomato plants	should be 1½–3 feet apart
" rows	should be 2–3 feet apart
Pepper plants	should be 1½–3 feet apart
" rows	should be 2 feet apart
Marigold plants	should be 1½ feet apart
" rows	should be 2 feet apart

SEEDS

To see how far apart the seeds should be planted,
look at the directions on the seed packet.

Beets	distance between rows should be 14–16 inches
Bush beans	" " " " " 2 feet
Carrots	" " " " " 14–16 inches
Loose-leaf lettuce	" " " " " 14–16 inches
Radishes	" " " " " 14–16 inches
Zucchini	" " " " " 4–5 feet

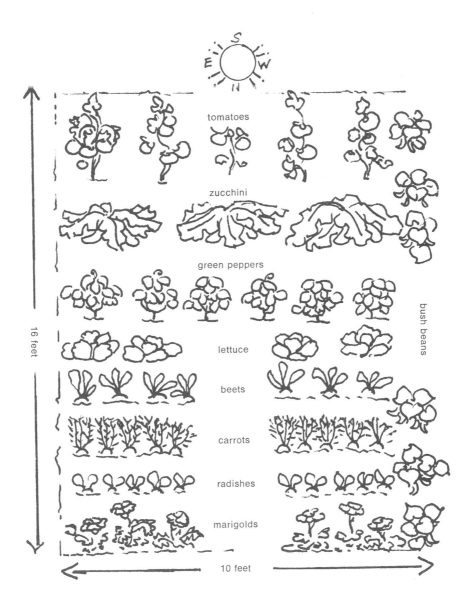

16 feet

10 feet

tomatoes

zucchini

green peppers

bush beans

lettuce

beets

carrots

radishes

marigolds

S
E · W
N

A KITCHEN GARDEN

This is a more-people-the-merrier family project. Grow marigolds (they help keep away some kinds of harmful bugs), tomatos, zucchini, green peppers, bush beans, lettuce, beets, carrots, and radishes. No other vegetables look lovelier or taste better than freshly picked ones that you have grown yourself!

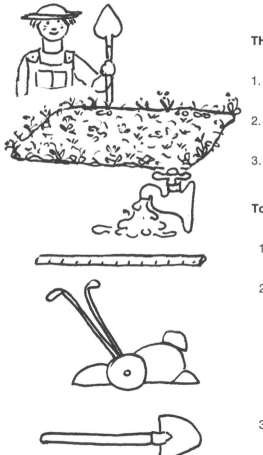

THINGS YOU WILL NEED

1. A least one helpful grown-up

2. A 10 x 16 foot piece of land

3. A near-at-hand water supply

Tools

1. A yardstick or tape measure

2. A rotary tiller (this is a gasoline-powered tool that looks somewhat like a lawn mower. It loosens, breaks up, and turns over the soil to get it ready for planting. It would be a big help but it is *not a necessity*)

3. A spade

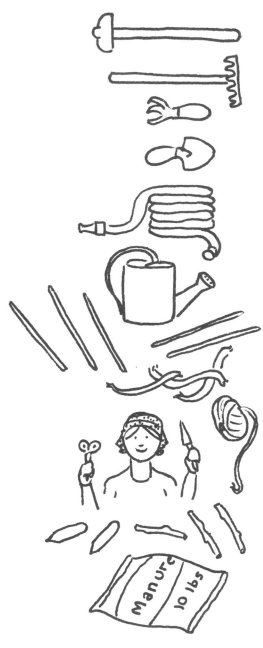

4. A hoe

5. A steel-tooth rake

6. A hand cultivator (a claw)

7. A trowel

8. A hose with a spray nozzle (a lawn soaker or sprinkler would be helpful but not necessary)

9. A watering can if you don't have a hose

10. 5 wooden or bamboo stakes

11. Ties—torn sheets or other soft rags torn in strips

12. String

13. Scissors or a knife, and a grown-up to use them

14. Sticks or garden markers

15. Fertilizer, such as well-rotted manure—about ten pounds

Plants

5 tomato plants

6 green pepper plants

6 dwarf marigold plants

Seeds

1 packet each: bush beans, zucchini, radish, loose-leaf lettuce, beets, carrots

PLANNING YOUR KITCHEN GARDEN

1. Choose the patch of land for your garden. It should be in a sunny area with soil that drains well. A garden won't grow in boggy soil.

2. You need to know just what the soil in your patch will require in the way of fertilizers and nutrients to make your garden flourish. Finding out is an interesting project all on its own.

HOW TO GO ABOUT IT

Almost every county in the United States has an Agricultural Division of the Cooperative Extension Offices. At each office there are very helpful people who will tell you how to go about getting a soil-testing kit (it costs about two dollars) and how to use it. After you have used the kit, the Extension Office will then tell you exactly what to add to the soil of your patch to make it fertile. The people at these offices also know the answer to just about any indoor or outdoor gardening question you may have. To find these people look up the name of your county in the phone book. There, along with many other offices, you will find listed either the Cooperative Extension Office or Service, or simply the Extension Service or Office. These offices exist for city-dwellers as well as suburban and country people. Give them a call. They are there to help people just like you.

GETTING READY TO PLANT

1. Clear the land of rocks and sticks and whatever else may be in the way.

2. Measure the desired area with a tape measure or yard-stick. Mark off the land by putting a stick firmly into the ground at each corner of the patch. Tie and stretch a string around the sticks to make an outline.

3. It is now time to till or dig the land to a depth of 4 inches. Turn the soil over, breaking up the clods as you go. You will need a strong back and a good spade for this work. Several willing workers would make the job a lot easier, but easiest of all would be to have an adult with a (rented, borrowed, or bought) rotary tiller do all the tilling and turning.

4. After the ground has been tilled and turned, scatter over the patch the fertilizer and whatever else you have discovered the soil needs. Turn these under, using either a rotary tiller or a spade.
   If you did not have your soil tested, ask a knowledgeable neighborhood gardener what he uses. Failing that, the odds are that you can't go wrong if you sprinkle the tilled area with ten pounds of well-rotted manure and turn it under.

5. Break up remaining clods of soil with a hoe.

6. Rake the soil to make it level.

PLANTING

1. The first seeds to plant will be the lettuce. They can be planted four weeks before the first *frost-free date* in your area. How do you find out this frost-free date? Those helpful Extension Service people know the date for the area in which you live and will share this information with you. Next plant the beet, carrot, and radish seeds two weeks before the frost-free date. The bean and zucchini seeds and green pepper plants can go in the ground one or two weeks after the frost-free date. The tomato plants should be planted no earlier than two weeks after the first frost-free date.

2. Mark each row before you plant it by stretching a string between two sticks or garden markers stuck in the ground at each end of the row. Marking helps you make straight rows and also shows where seeds have been planted. Use the string as a guide when making furrows with your finger, trowel, or a stick.

3. Plant the seeds following the directions on the seed packet. The packet will tell you how far apart and at what depth the seeds should be planted. Use a ruler or yardstick to aid you.

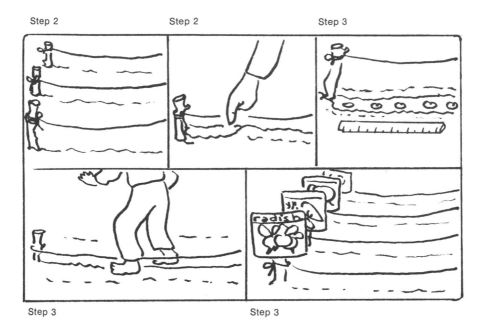

After you have planted each row of seeds, firmly press down the soil over the seeds, so they won't wash away when watered. Use either your foot or the back of a trowel to do this. Put the name of the seeds you have planted at the end of each row. The empty seed packet can be slipped over the marker at the end of the row. The string is usually left up until the plants have sprouted to show that the area has been planted. It can be removed any time after that.

4. Plants that have been started in plastic or clay pots must be unpotted before planting. To make this easy, water the plants first, then holding the main stem of the plant between two fingers of one hand and the pot in the other hand, turn the plant upside down and slip the pot from

the plant. If it doesn't come off easily try this: still holding the pot and plant in the upside down position, rap the rim of the pot a couple of times against the edge of a porch or a step or something similar. Now lift the pot off the plant. If the plants come in a flat (a box holding several plants), they will need to be cut apart with a sharp knife. Slice through the soil, leaving each plant an equal amount of earth. Simply lift each plant from the flat. Dig little holes in the garden deep enough to hold the plant roots.

Put one plant in each hole and press the soil down firmly to hold them securely.

Check the Garden Planning Chart (page 74) to see how much space you should leave between the plants and rows.

5. Push a stake into the ground behind each tomato plant.

6. Water the freshly planted seeds and plants thoroughly. Spray gently, using a hose with a spray nozzle, or sprinkle slowly and carefully, using a watering can.

Step 4

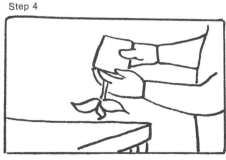

Step 4

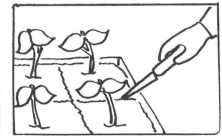

Tending the Kitchen Garden

WATERING

A vegetable garden needs at least one inch of rain a week.
Since it often does not rain that much every week, you will
probably need to water. Give your garden an hour-long
soaking two or three times a week. A long soaking every so
often is much better for plants than short, daily sprinkles.
When vegetables are about ready to be picked, water the
plants more frequently. A plant that wilts when its fruit is
heavy will not recover.

THINNING

The first signs of little green plants will show above the
ground anywhere from one to three weeks after the seeds
were planted. Growing plants need breathing and growing
room. However, they tend to crowd each other. Help them
out by first thinning them so they are at least a quarter of
an inch apart. Do this by pulling out all extra plants when
they are large enough to hold onto, then toss them away.
Later on, when they seem to be crowding each other again,
thin the plants once more, leaving as much space between
them as indicated in the instructions on the packet
of seeds.

Give the lettuce and beets their second thinning when they
are still small, yet large enough to eat. The lettuce makes

a delicious and delicate salad. The tiny, thinned-out beets are good when steamed—root, leaf, and all.

Toss out all the other plants removed during the second thinning. They are not good to eat.

TYING-BACK

Using soft rags, loosely tie the tomato plants to the stakes when they begin to droop. Tying-back keeps the fruit off the ground so it does not spoil.

WEEDING

Weeds are real troublemakers. Bugs live in them, they harbor diseases, and they use up much of the water and many of the nutrients your vegetables need to flourish. To keep them under control, hoe between the rows and around the larger plants as soon as the weeds appear. Use a hand cultivator (claw) around the smaller plants. Be careful not to hoe or cultivate too deeply—the roots of your vegetable plants are very delicate and damage easily.

INSECTS AND BUGS

Many bugs, such as lightning bugs, ladybugs, and praying mantises are garden friends. They eat the bugs that eat the plants. Unfortunately, however, many other bugs enjoy vegetables as much as we do. One way of getting rid of them is to pick them off the plants, then squash them or drop them into a jar of soapy water. Another way is to spray or dust the plants with one of the many insect repellents sold by hardware stores and garden centers. These stores also sell fungicides and other products that control plant disease. Be sure that the product you buy is safe to use in vegetable gardens. Some garden products are poisonous; the label will tell you if they are.

THE HARVEST

How long it will take until the vegetables are ripe enough to pick depends a great deal on the weather. Below, however, is the approximate number of weeks between the planting of seeds and the harvesting of vegetables.

Beets	8	weeks
Bush Beans	11	,,
Carrots	10	,,
Cucumbers	11	,,
Lettuce	5	,,
Radishes	3½	,,
Zucchini	8–9	,,

Tomatoes and peppers will be ready two months or more after the plants have been placed in the garden.

Vegetables taste best when they are young and tender and when they have been picked just a few minutes before cooking and eating.

The plants are less likely to be damaged by picking if you harvest the vegetables by cutting them off with a sharp knife rather than pulling them off.

If you harvest more vegetables than you can use right away, keep them in the refrigerator or, better still, share them with a friend, and you'll both feel happy.

AN HERB GARDEN

Herbs are used for making things smell and taste good, for keeping bugs away, for making magic potions, dying cloth, curing ailments, and making lovely gardens.

For many centuries herbs have been grown in gardens that form charming patterns and designs.

Here is a simple pattern for a small herb garden of your own.

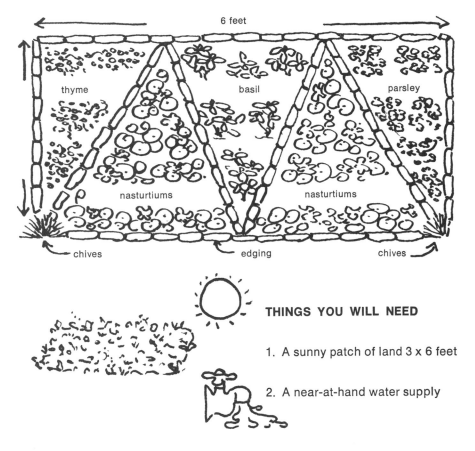

6 feet

thyme

basil

parsley

nasturtiums

nasturtiums

chives   edging   chives

THINGS YOU WILL NEED

1. A sunny patch of land 3 x 6 feet

2. A near-at-hand water supply

3. Large pebbles, stones, bricks, shells, or weathered strips of wood, etc.

4. A yardstick or tape measure

5. String

6. Scissors or a knife and a grown-up to use them

Tools

1. A spade

2. A steel-tooth rake

3. A trowel

4. A hose with a spray nozzle or a watering can

Plants

2 chive

4 thyme

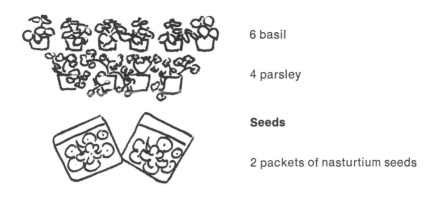

6 basil

4 parsley

Seeds

2 packets of nasturtium seeds

PLANNING YOUR HERB GARDEN

Choose a patch of land 3 x 6 feet with soil that drains well. This patch should be in a bright spot that gets two or more hours of sun a day, the more sun the better.

It would be nice if you could find a patch like this next to a stone wall or a fence. They make good-looking backgrounds for herb gardens.

GETTING READY TO PLANT

1. Clear the land of rocks, sticks, roots, or whatever else may be in the way.

2. Measure and mark off the patch of land by putting a stick firmly into the ground at each corner. Tie and stretch a string around the sticks to make an outline.

3. Now comes a job for someone fairly strong. Dig the soil to a depth of 4 inches. Turn the soil over as you go.

4. With the edge of the spade break up the clods of newly turned soil to the size of big pebbles.

5. Rake the soil to make it level.

6. Before planting, mark off the pattern of the herb garden. Do this the same way you marked off the patch itself, this time adding a marking stick plunk in the middle of the front border and two more sticks two feet in from each end of the back border. Now tie and stretch the string back and forth around the sticks to form a zigzag triangular pattern.

MAKING AN EDGING

Your herb garden will look very special if you make an edging for it, using bricks, stones, shells, or strips of weathered wood. Place them all around the border of the patch and along the outline of the zigzaggy pattern.

You may now remove the strings if you like.

PLANTING

1. Plant the nasturtium seeds (they will take two to three weeks to sprout) after all danger of frost is past. Your county Cooperative Extension Office will gladly tell you the safest planting times in your area. See page 80 in the Kitchen Garden chapter for more about this.

Following the herb garden pattern:

2. Plant herbs that came in peat moss pots, pots and all. Using a trowel, dig little holes in the ground just deep enough to hold each pot, then press the earth firmly around them.

    If the herbs come in plastic or clay pots, they must be unpotted before planting. To make this easy, water the plants first. Then holding the main stem of the plant between two fingers of one hand and the pot in the other, turn the plant upside down and slip the pot from the plant. If it doesn't come off easily, try this: still holding the pot and plant in the upside-down position, rap the rim of the pot a couple of times against the edge of something solid, like a garden table. Now lift the pot off the plant. If the plants come in a flat, they will need to be cut apart with a sharp knife. Slice through the soil, leaving each plant an equal amount of earth. Simply lift each plant from the flat.

    Dig little holes in the ground deep enough to hold the plants' roots. Put one plant in each hole and firmly press down the soil around them.

3. Plant the nasturtium seeds following the directions on the packet. The packet will tell you how far apart to place the rows and at what depth the seeds should be planted. Use a ruler or yardstick to help you.

4. Water the freshly planted seeds and herbs thoroughly. Spray gently, using a hose with a spray nozzle, or sprinkle slowly and carefully, using a watering can.

Tending the Herb Garden

WATERING

Herbs need very little water. Water them about once a week if it doesn't rain.

WEEDING

The herb garden is small and easily weeded by hand. Weed when the soil is moist. It's easier that way. Pull out the weeds very carefully so the herbs are not uprooted, too.

HARVESTING

When the plants begin to look strong and healthy, snip off sprigs of herbs as you need them. You can use a knife or scissors to do this.

Nasturtium leaves should be ready about two months after planting. Toss them into salads. Sprinkle chives over cottage cheese, add thyme to stews, eat basil with tomatoes, and use parsley with almost anything.

On a warm summer evening you might try brushing your hand very, very gently back and forth over the thyme. A magnificent cloud of fragrance will float up to you.

GLOSSARY

Claw Looks like a small, short, rake with three curved fingers or claws. Use it to loosen the dirt around your garden plants.

Fertilizer Vegetable, animal, or chemical food you can use to help your plants grow bigger, healthier, and more fruitful.

Flat A shallow, rectangular box that holds, usually, a dozen or so young plants.

Frost-free date That day, in your area, when all danger of frost is considered to be past and it is safe to put in your first seeds and plants.

Furrow A shallow trench in the soil in which you plant your seeds.

Insecticide A spray or powder you put on plants to discourage and/or kill insects that might eat them.

Peat Moss (also *sphagnum moss*) Decayed mosses used as an ingredient in potting soil to make it more porous.

Perlite (also *vermiculite*) Lightweight, inorganic materials used as ingredients in potting soil to help it absorb excess moisture and "breathe" more easily.

Potting soil   A specially prepared soil, dark and crumbly, porous and workable, that contains all the nutrients and minerals your plant needs. You can buy it or make it.

Vermiculite   See Perlite.